PIANO · VOCAL · GUITAR

ETERNAL GLORY

Songs for Memorial Services WITHDRAWN

ISBN 0-634-03010-8

HAL•LEONARD®
CORPORATION
7777 W. BLUEMOUND RD. P.O. BOX 13819 MILWAUKEE, WI 53213

Visit Hal Leonard Online at
www.halleonard.com

ABIDE WITH ME

Words by HENRY F. LYTE
Music by WILLIAM H. MONK

AMAZING GRACE

Words by JOHN NEWTON
Traditional American Melody

lost, but now _____ am ____ found, was blind, but ____
brought me safe _____ thus ____ far, and grace will ____
sess with - in _____ the ____ veil a life of ____

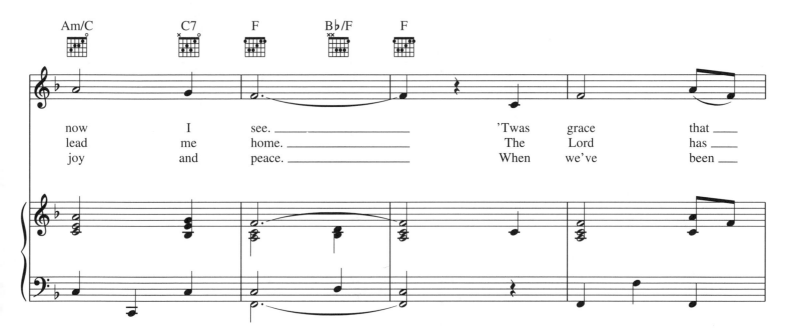

now I see. _____ 'Twas grace that ____
lead me home. _____ The Lord has ____
joy and peace. _____ When we've been ____

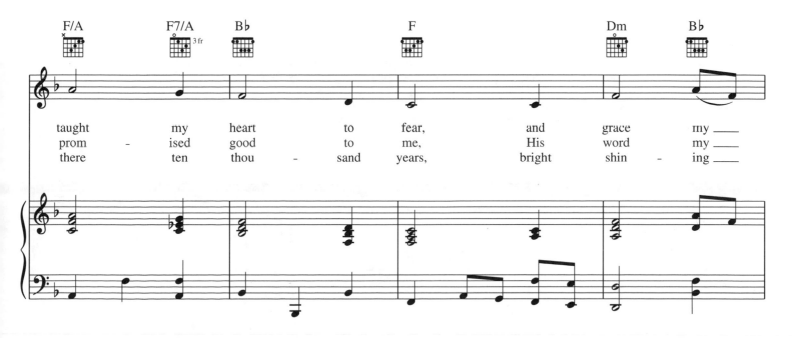

taught my heart to fear, and grace my ____
prom - ised good to me, His word my ____
there ten thou - sand years, bright shin - ing ____

BECAUSE HE LIVES

Words by WILLIAM J. and GLORIA GAITHER
Music by WILLIAM J. GAITHER

Lyrics:

Verse

God sent His Son, _____ they called him Je - sus; _____
hold _____ our new - born ba - by, _____

_____ He came to love, _____ heal and for -
_____ And came feel the pride _____ and joy He

give; _____ He lived and died _____
gives; _____ But great - er still _____

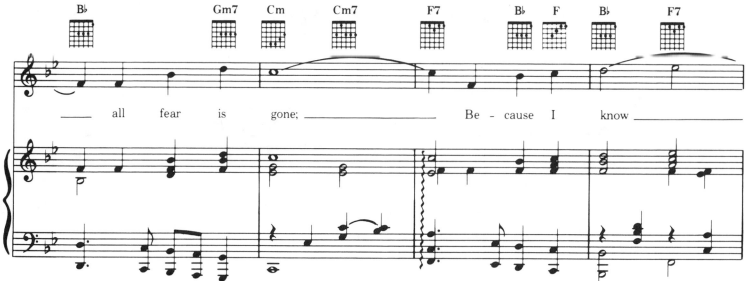

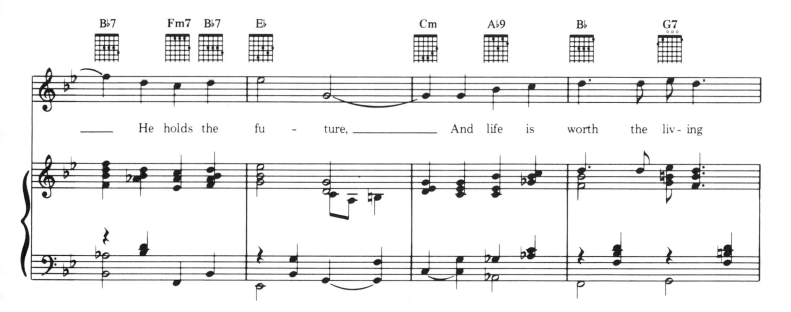

3. And then one day I'll cross that river;
   I'll fight life's final war with pain;
   And then as death gives way to vict'ry,
   I'll see the lights of glory and I'll know He reigns.

AVE MARIA

By FRANZ SCHUBERT

A - - ve Ma - ri -
A - - ve Ma - ri -

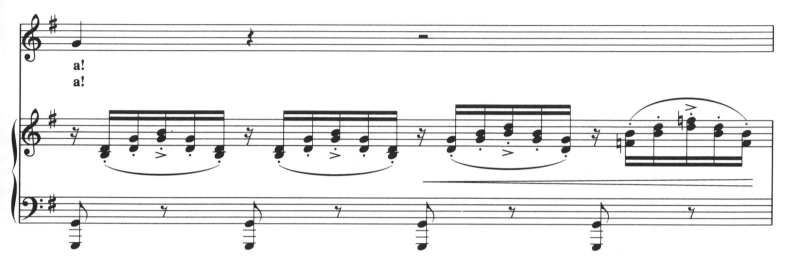

a!
a!

dim.

BEAUTIFUL ISLE OF SOMEWHERE

Words by JESSIE B. POUNDS
Music by JOHN S. FEARIS

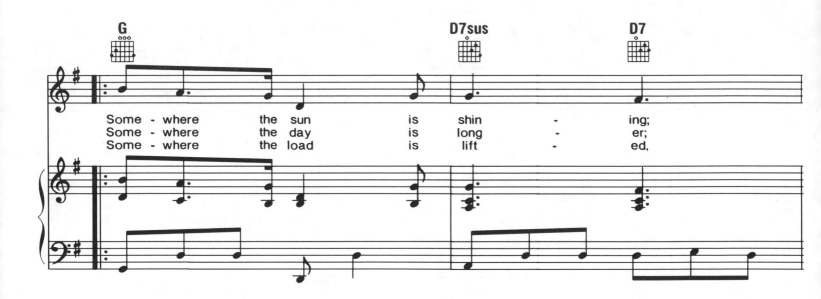

Some-where the sun is shin - ing;
Some-where the day is long - er;
Some-where the load is lift - ed,

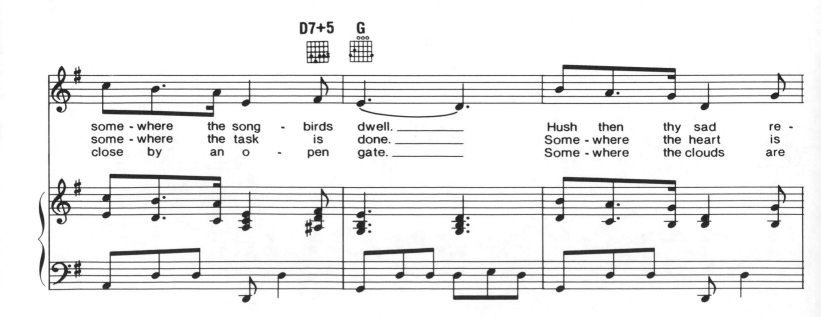

some-where the song - birds dwell. _____ Hush then thy sad re -
some-where the task is done. _____ Some-where the heart is
close by an o - pen gate. _____ Some-where the clouds are

BLESSED ASSURANCE

Lyrics by FANNY J. CROSBY
Music by PHOEBE PALMER KNAPP

With movement

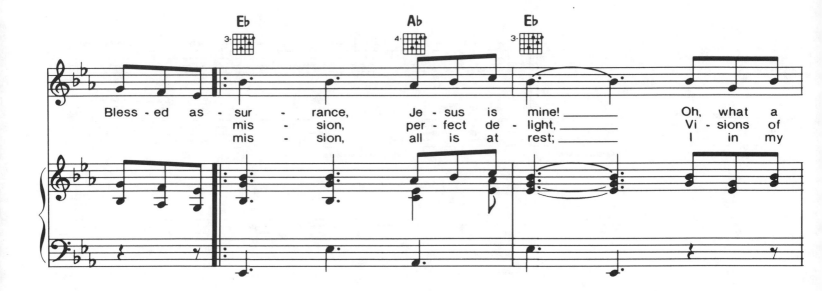

Bless- ed as - sur - rance, Je - sus is mine! _____ Oh, what a
mis - sion, per - fect de - light, _____ Vi - sions of
mis - sion, all is at rest; _____ I in my

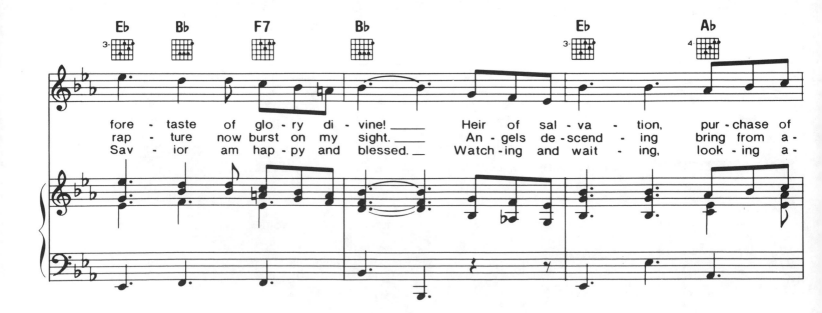

fore - taste of glo - ry di - vine! _____ Heir of sal - va - tion, pur - chase of
rap - ture now burst on my sight. _____ An - gels de - scend - ing bring from a -
Sav - ior am hap - py and blessed. _____ Watch - ing and wait - ing, look - ing a -

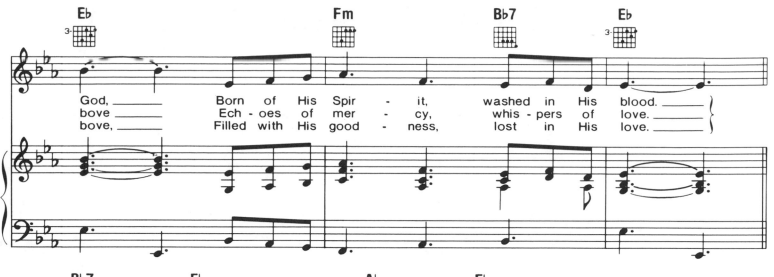

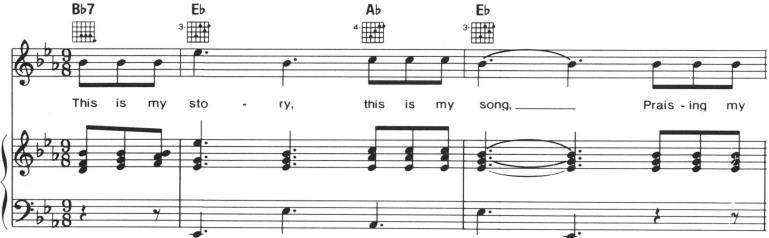

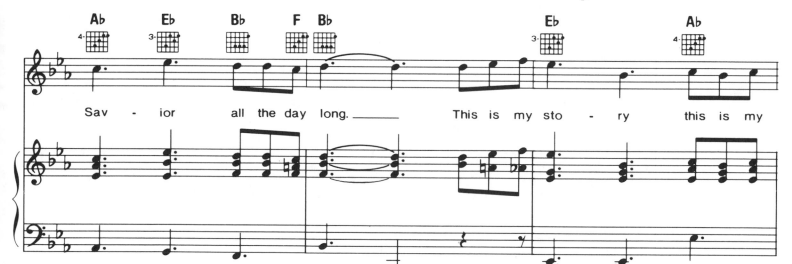

DEEP RIVER

African-American Spiritual
Based on Joshua 3

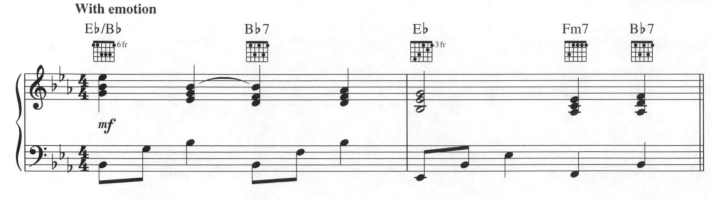

With emotion

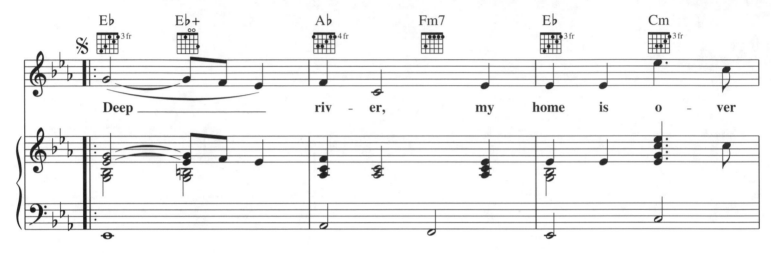

Deep _____ riv - er, my home is o - ver

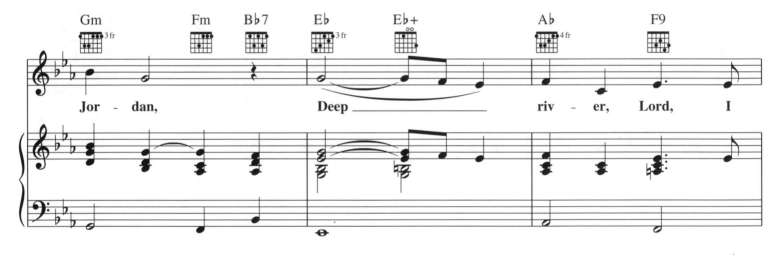

Jor - dan, Deep _____ riv - er, Lord, I

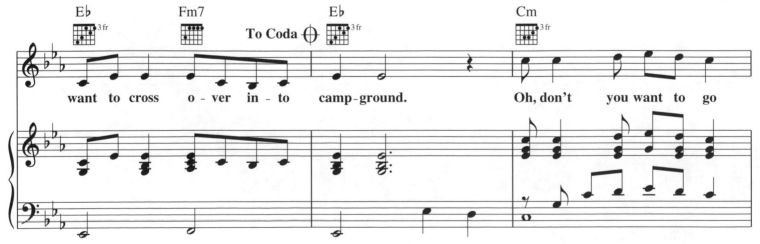

want to cross o - ver in - to camp-ground. Oh, don't you want to go

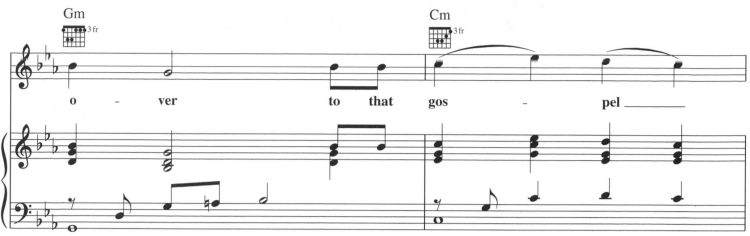

o - ver to that gos - pel

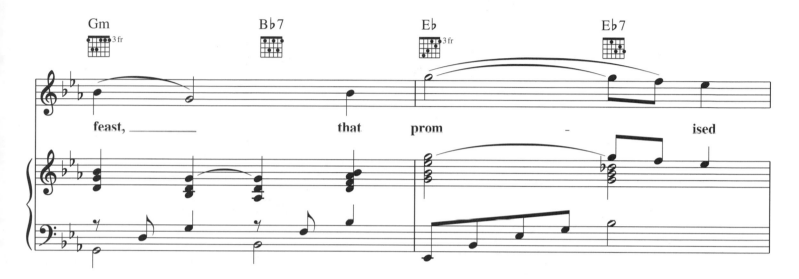

feast, that prom - ised

D.S. al Coda

land where all is peace. Oh,

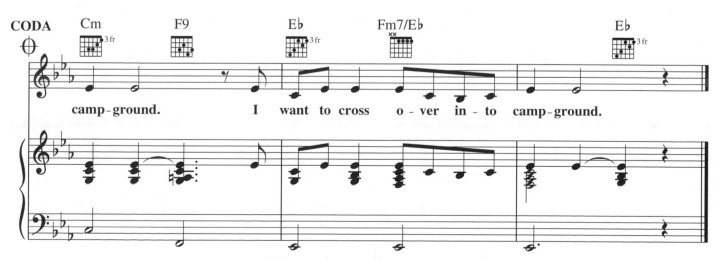

camp-ground. I want to cross o - ver in - to camp-ground.

DOES JESUS CARE?

Words by FRANK E. GRAEFF
Music by J. LINCOLN HALL

long? _____
near? _____
long? _____
see? _____

O yes, He cares, I know He cares; His

heart is touched with my grief. _____ When the days are wea - ry, the

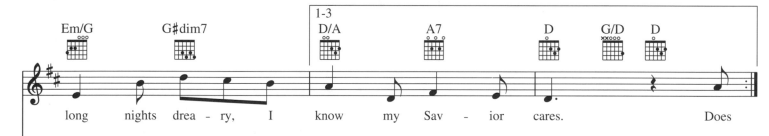

long nights drea - ry, I know my Sav - ior cares. Does

know my Sav - ior cares. I know my Sav - ior cares.

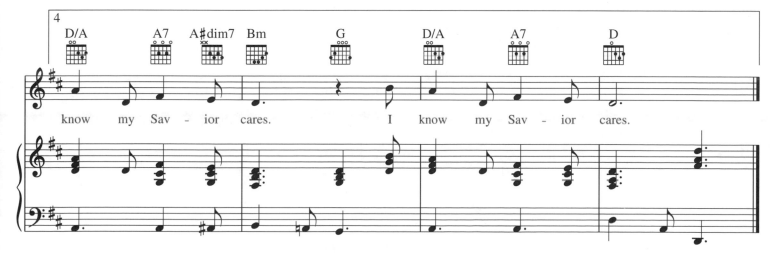

FOR ALL THE SAINTS

Words by WILLIAM W. HOW
Music by RALPH VAUGHAN WILLIAMS

Stately

For all the saints   who from their la - bors rest,   who
Thou wast their Rock,   their For - tress, and their Might;
O may Thy sol - diers, faith - ful, true and bold,
O blest com - mu - nion, fel - low - ship di - vine!

Thee   by faith be - fore the world con - fessed,   Thy
Thou, Lord, their faith Cap - tain   in the well - fought fight.
fight as the saints who no - bly fought of old,   and
We fee - bly strug - gle; they in glo - ry shine.   Yet

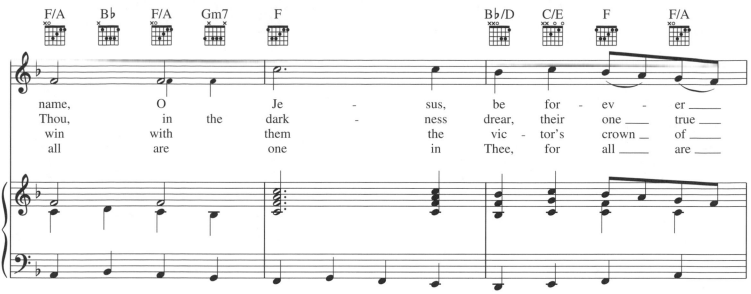

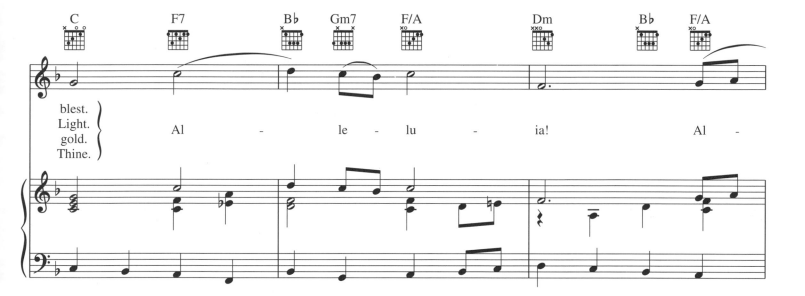

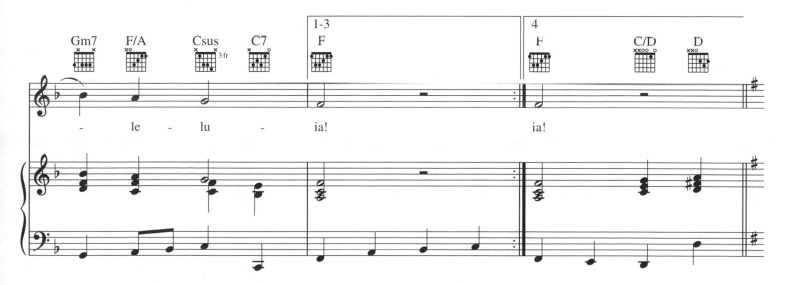

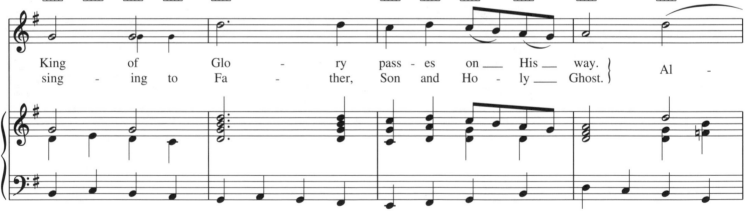

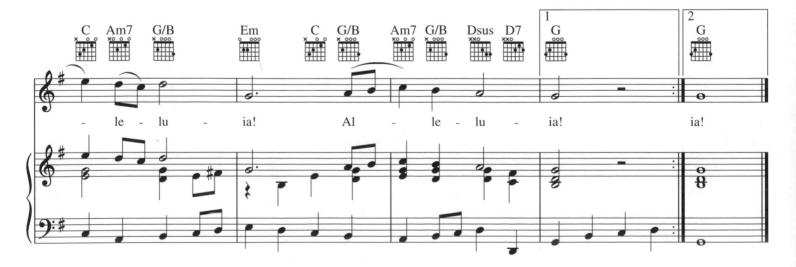

FRIENDS

Recorded by Michael W. Smith

Words and Music by MICHAEL W. SMITH
and DEBORAH D. SMITH

GIVE ME JESUS

African-American Spiritual

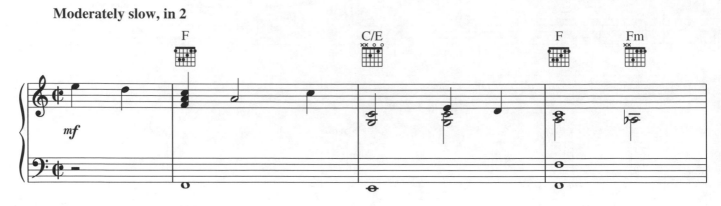

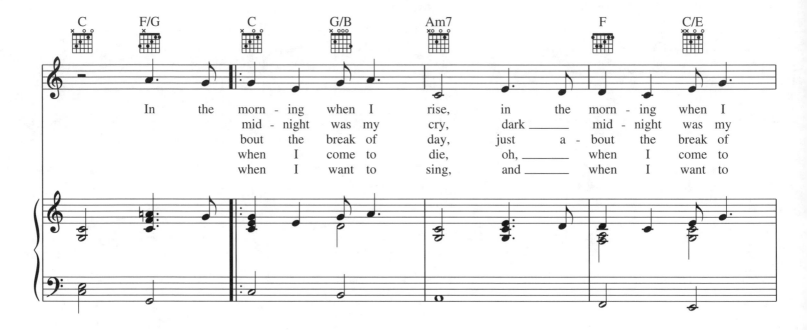

In the morn-ing when I rise, in the morn-ing when I
mid-night was my cry, dark _____ mid-night was my
bout the break of day, just a-bout the break of
when I come to die, oh, _____ when I come to
when I want to sing, and _____ when I want to

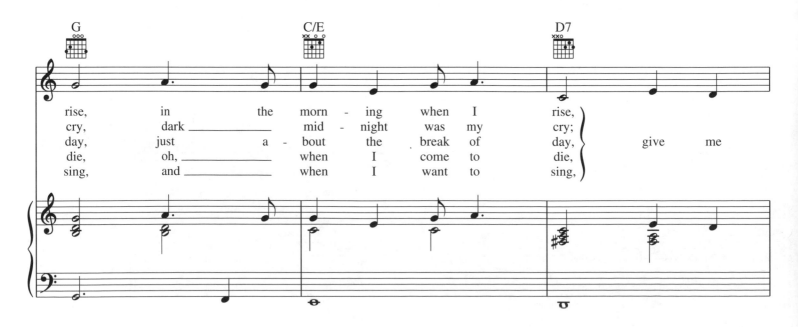

rise, in the morn-ing when I rise,
cry, dark _____ mid-night was my cry;
day, just a-bout the break of day, give me
die, oh, _____ when I come to die,
sing, and _____ when I want to sing,

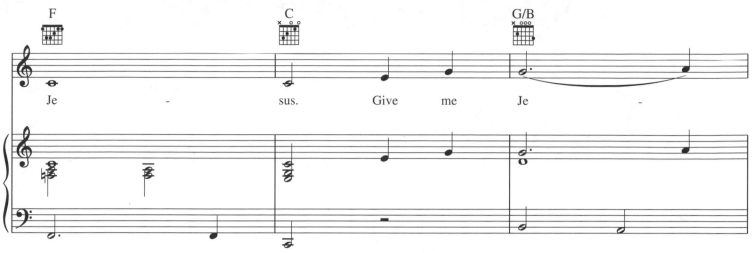

Je - sus. Give me Je -

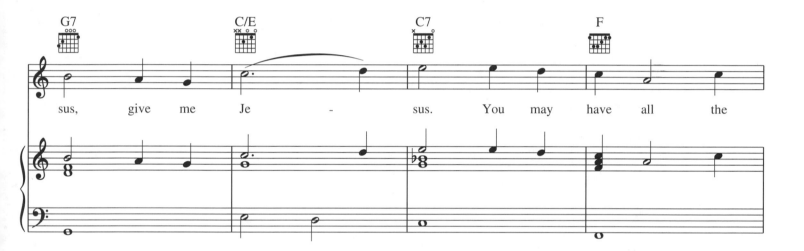

sus, give me Je - sus. You may have all the

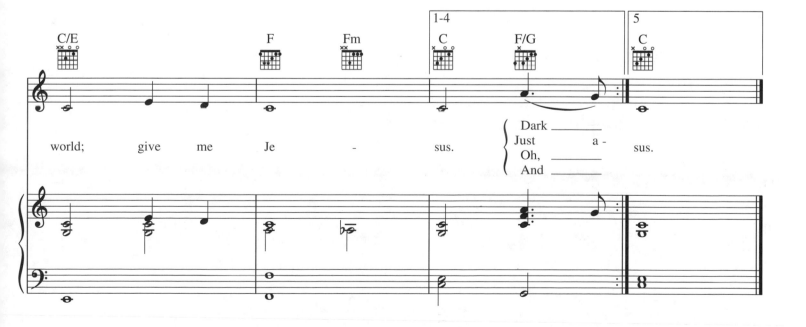

world; give me Je - sus.

Dark _____
Just a - sus.
Oh, _____
And _____

HE SHALL FEED HIS FLOCK

Text adapted from the Book of Isaiah, 40:11
Music by GEORGE FRIDERIC HANDEL

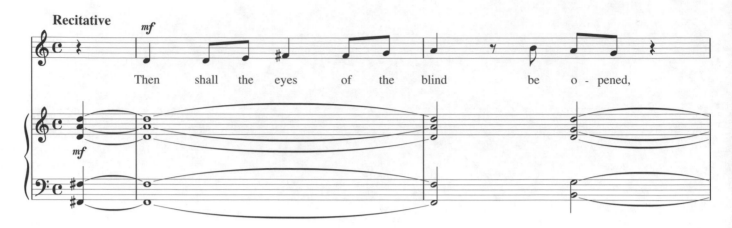

and car - ry ____ them ____ in His bo - som, and

gent - ly lead ____ those ____ that are ____ with young, ____ and

gent - ly lead ____ those, ____ and gent - ly lead ____ those that

are ____ with young.

HOW GREAT THOU ART

Words and Music by
STUART K. HINE

*Author's original words are "works" and "mighty."

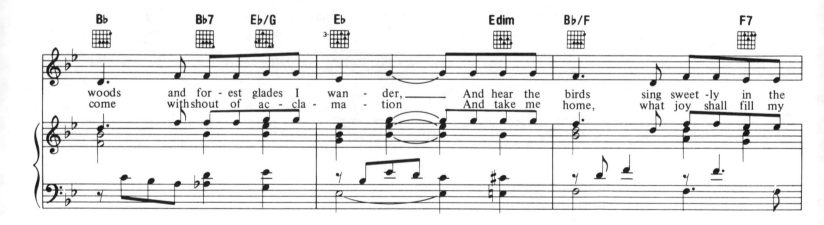

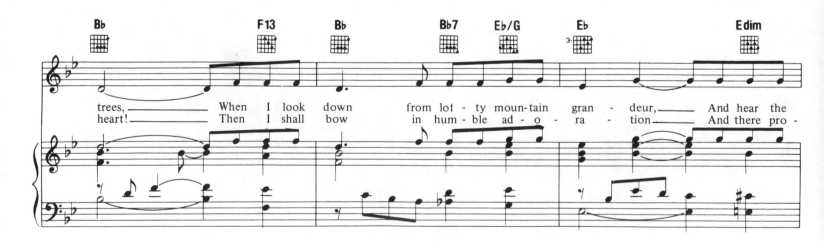

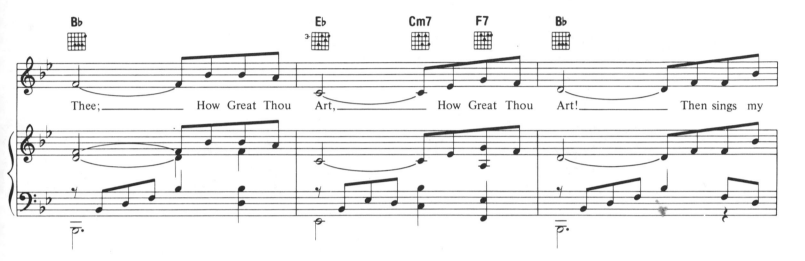

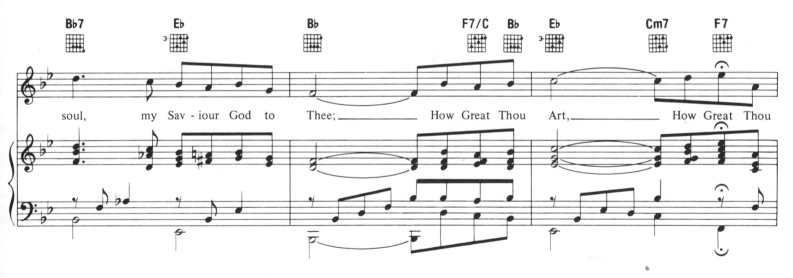

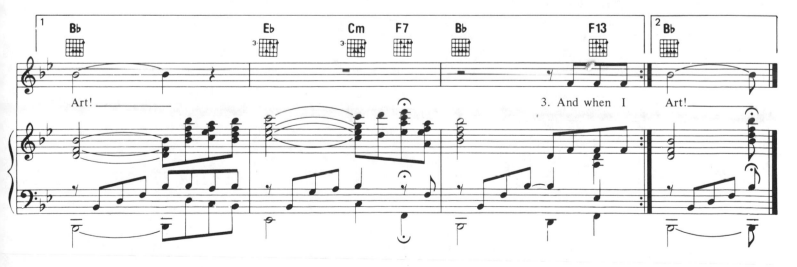

HE THE PEARLY GATES WILL OPEN

Words by FREDRICK A. BLOM
Translated by NATHANIEL CARLSON
Music by ELSIE AHLWEN

Love di-vine, so great and won - drous, deep and might - y, pure, sub-lime,
Like a dove when hunt - ed, fright - ened, as a wound-ed fawn was I.
Love di-vine, so great and won - drous! All my sins He then for-gave.
In life's e - ven-tide, at twi - light, at His door I'll knock and wait.

com - ing from the heart of Je - sus, just the same through tests of time!
Bro - ken-heart - ed, yet He healed me; He will heed the sin - ner's cry.
I will sing His praise for - ev - er for His blood, His pow'r to save.
By the pre - cious love of Je - sus, I shall en - ter heav - en's gate.

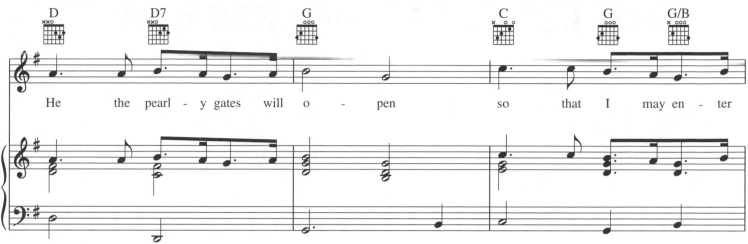

He the pearl - y gates will o - pen so that I may en - ter

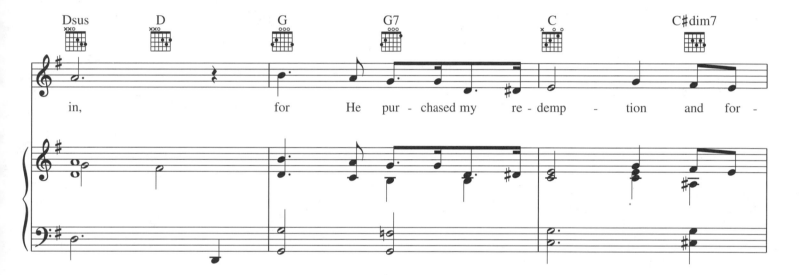

in, for He pur - chased my re - demp - tion and for -

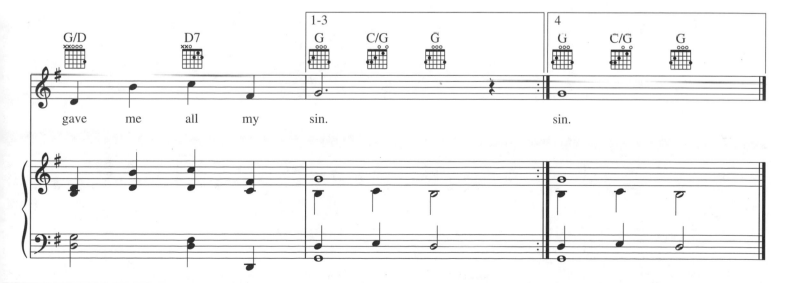

gave me all my sin. sin.

HIS EYE IS ON THE SPARROW

Words by CIVILLA D. MARTIN
Music by CHARLES H. GABRIEL

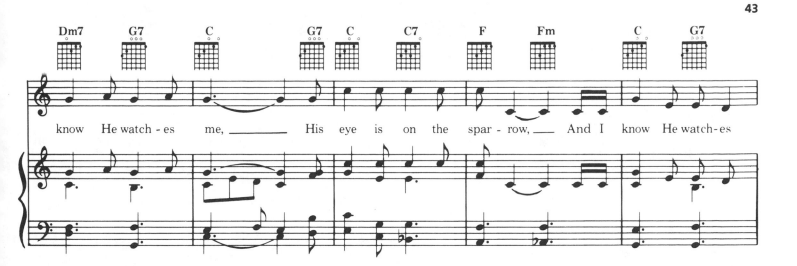

know He watch - es me, _____ His eye is on the spar - row, ___ And I know He watch-es

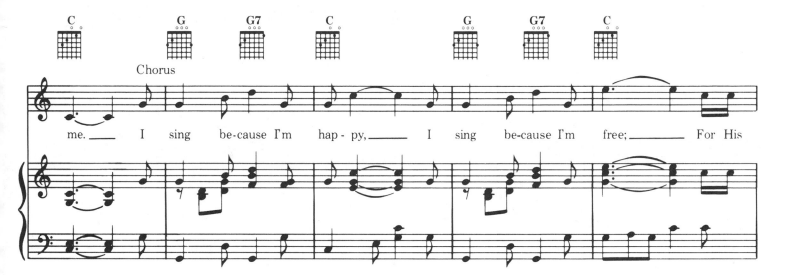

Chorus

me. ___ I sing be-cause I'm hap - py, _____ I sing be-cause I'm free; _____ For His

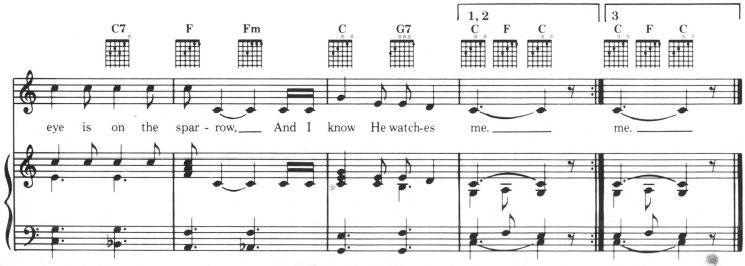

eye is on the spar - row, ___ And I know He watch-es me. _____ me. _____

3. Whenever I am tempted,
   Whenever clouds arise.
   When song gives place to sighing,
   When hope within me dies.
   I draw the closer to Him,
   From care He sets me free:

HOME FREE
Recorded by Wayne Watson

Words and Music by
WAYNE WATSON

Easy ♩ = 80

1. I'm try - ing

hard not to think You un-kind,_____ but Heav-en-ly Fa-

-ther,_____ if You know my heart, sure-ly You can read my mind.

Good peo-ple un-der-neath a sea of grief. Some

get up and walk_ a-way,_____ some will find ul-ti-mate re-lief._____

Home free,—— e - ven - tu - al - ly;—— at the

ul - ti - mate—— heal - ing we will be home—— free.—— Home free,—— oh,

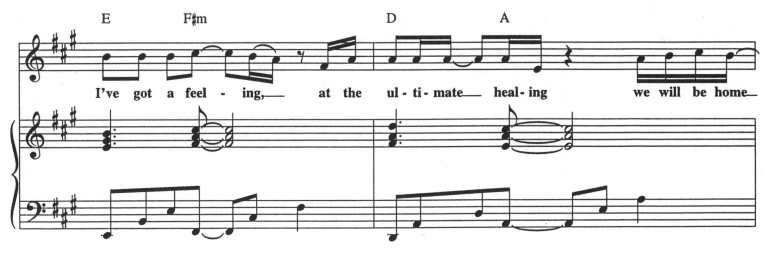

I've got a feel - ing,—— at the ul - ti - mate—— heal - ing we will be home——

free.——

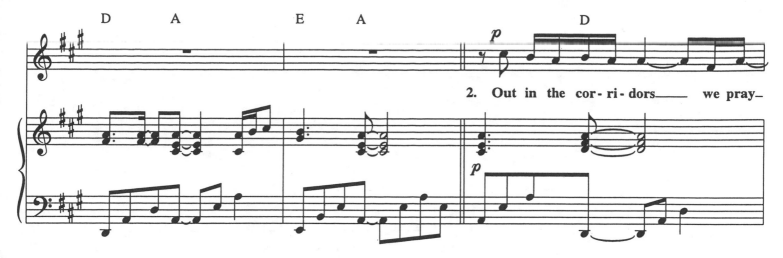

2. Out in the cor-ri-dors___ we pray___

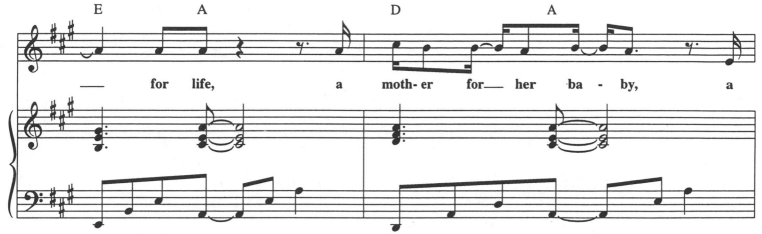

___ for life, a moth-er for___ her ba - by, a

hus-band for his wife.___ Oh,___ some-times the good___ die___ young; it's

sad but true. And while we pray for one more heart-beat, the real

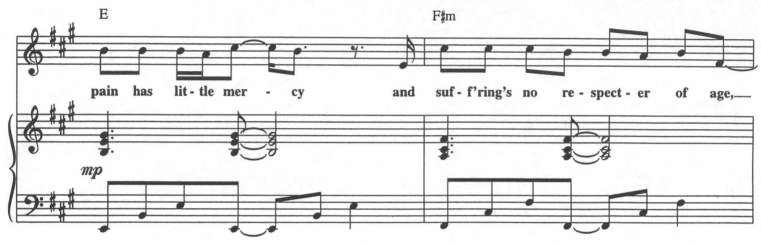

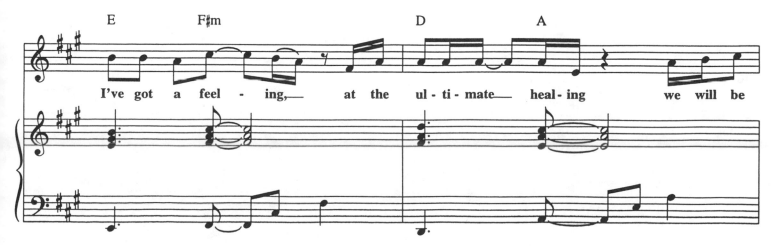

home free.___ Home free,___ e - ven - tu - al - ly;___ at the

ul - ti - mate___ heal - ing we will be home free.___ Home free,___ oh,

I've got a feel - ing,___ at the ul - ti - mate___ heal - ing we're gon - na be

home___ free.___ Home___

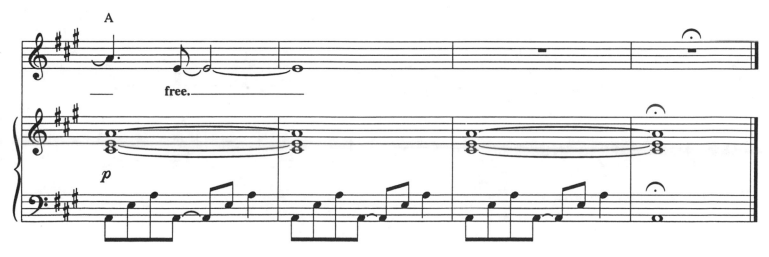

I WALKED TODAY WHERE JESUS WALKED

By GEOFFREY O'HARA
and DANIEL TWOHIG

* Words used by exclusive permission

lit - tle lanes, they have not changed— A sweet peace fills the

air. I walked to-day where Je- sus walked, _____ And

felt His pres- ence there. My

Allegretto

path-way led through Beth - le - hem, _____ Ah! mem-'ries

ev - - - er sweet; The

lit - tle hills of Gal - i - lee, _____ That knew those

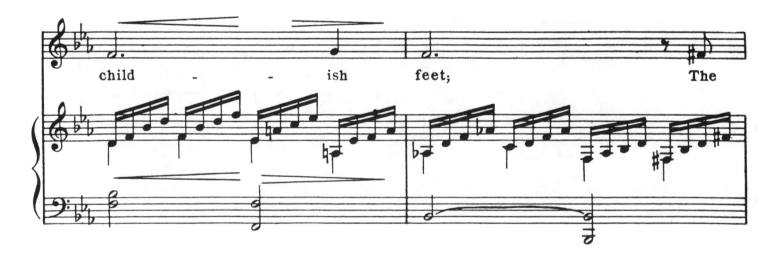

child - - ish feet; The

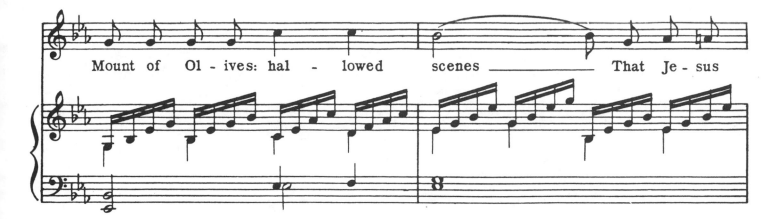

Mount of Ol - ives: hal - lowed scenes _____ That Je - sus

knew be - fore; I

saw the might - y Jor - dan roll _____ As in the

days of yore.

I knelt to-day where Je-sus knelt, ___ Where

all a-lone He prayed; The Gar - den of Geth-sem - a -

ne ___ My heart felt un - a - fraid! I

picked my heav-y bur-den up ___ And with Him by my

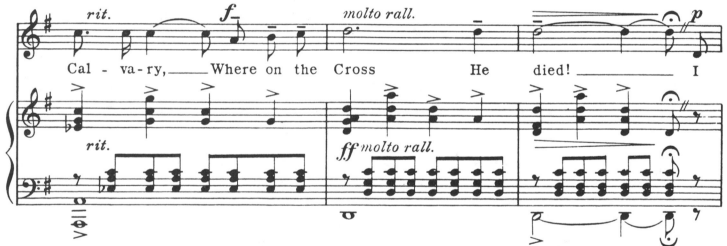

I'LL FLY AWAY

Words and Music by
ALBERT E. BRUMLEY

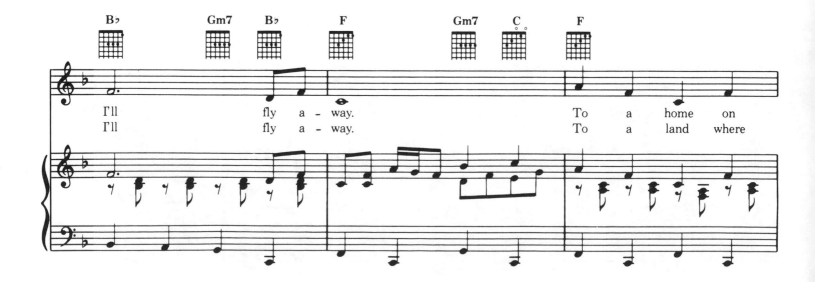

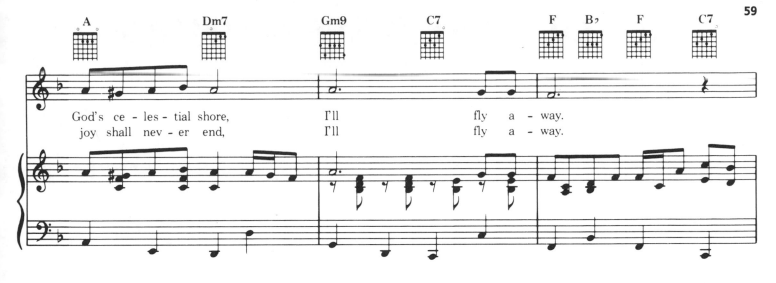

God's ce - les - tial shore,   I'll   fly   a - way.
joy shall nev - er end,   I'll   fly   a - way.

Chorus

I'll   fly   a - way,   O   glo - ry,   I'll   fly a -

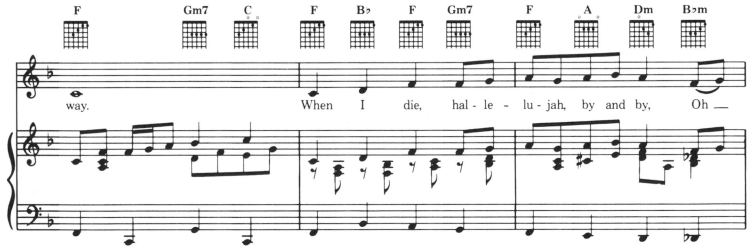

way.   When I   die, hal - le - lu - jah, by and by,   Oh ___

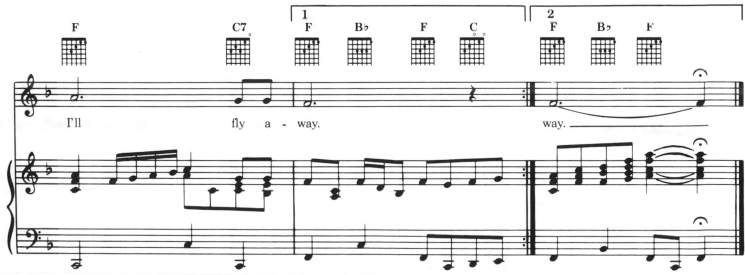

I'll   fly   a - way.   way. _____

IF YOU COULD SEE ME NOW

Recorded by Truth

Words and Music by
KIM NOBLITT

Very slowly and freely

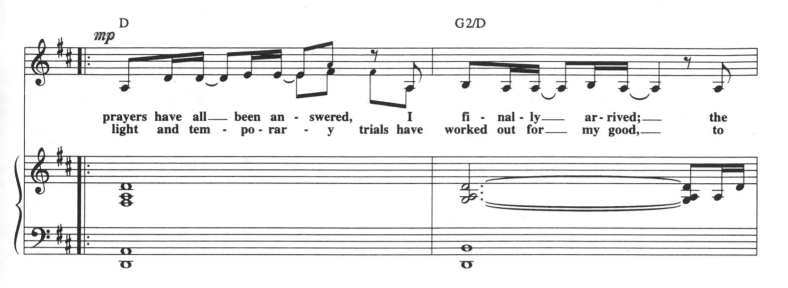

prayers have all__ been an - swered, I fi - nal - ly__ ar - rived;__ the
light and tem - po - rar - y trials have worked out for__ my good,__ to

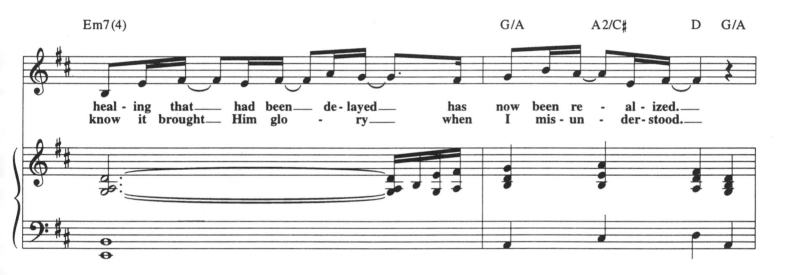

heal - ing that__ had been__ de - layed__ has now been re - al - ized.__
know it brought__ Him glo - ry__ when I mis - un - der - stood.__

No one's in__ a hur - ry, there's no sched - ule__ to__ keep;__ we're
Though we've had__ our sor - rows, they can nev - er__ com - pare.__ What

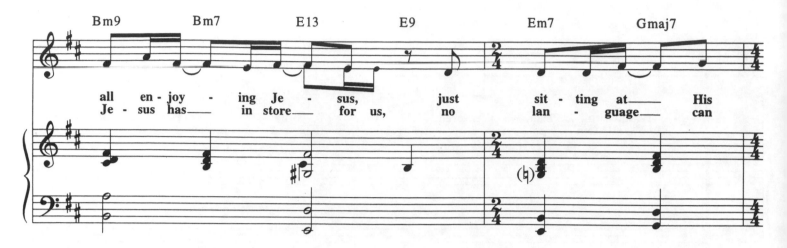

all en - joy - ing Je - sus, just sit - ting at____ His
Je - sus has____ in store for us, no lan - guage____ can

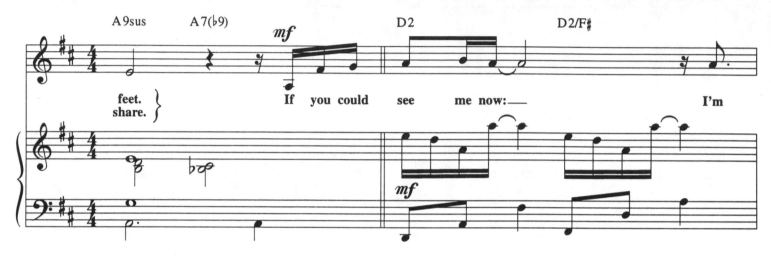

feet.
share.

If you could see me now:____ I'm

walk - ing streets____ of gold.____ If you could see me now:____ I'm

stand - ing tall____ and whole.____ If you could see me now,_____ you'd

know I've seen His face. If you could see me now,_____ you'd

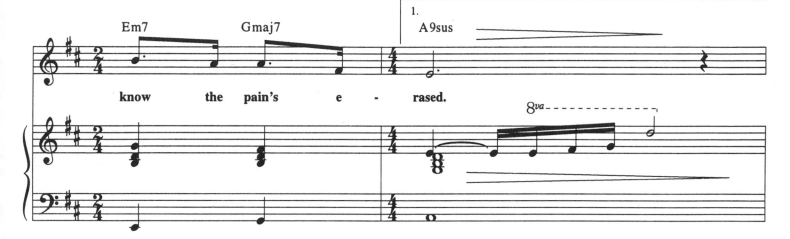

know the pain's e - rased.

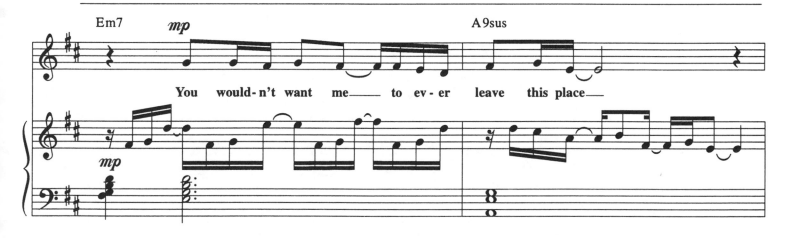

You would-n't want me___ to ev - er leave this place___

if you___ could on - ly see___ me now. My

N.C.

me now,

if you could on - ly

very slowly and freely

p

see me now. now.

gradually slowing to end

p *p*

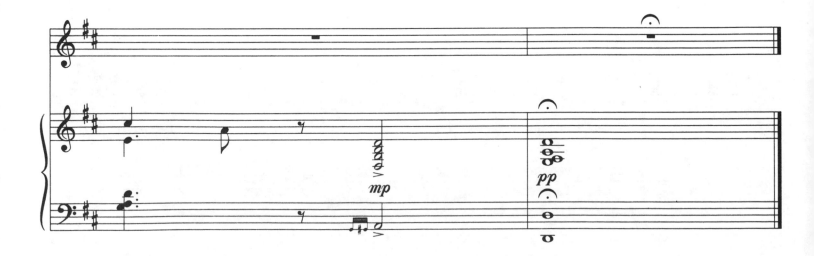

mp

pp

IVORY PALACES

Words and Music by
HENRY BARRACLOUGH

world of woe; _____ on - ly His

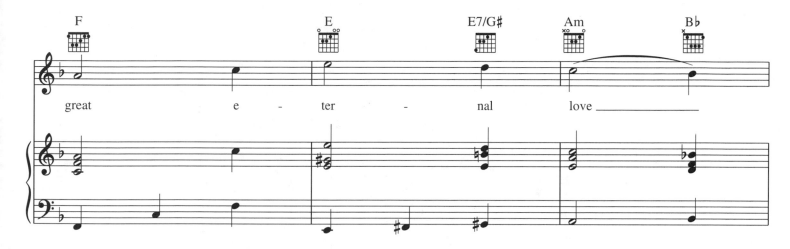

great e - ter - nal love _____

made _____ my Sav - ior go. _____

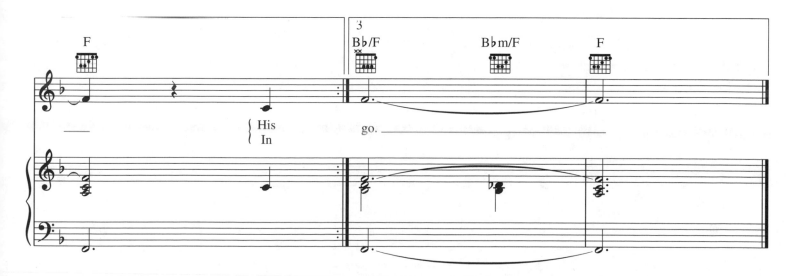

His _____ go. _____
In

IN THE GARDEN

Words and Music by
C. AUSTIN MILES

IT IS WELL WITH MY SOUL

Words by HORATIO G. SPAFFORD
Music by PHILIP P. BLISS

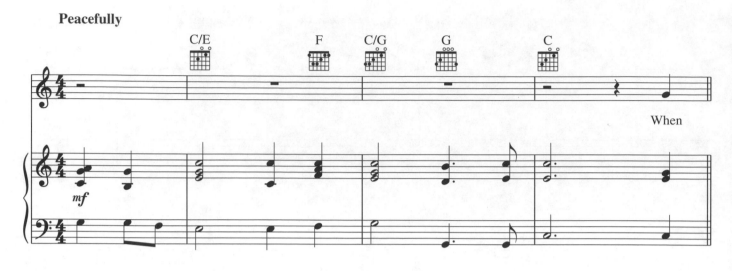

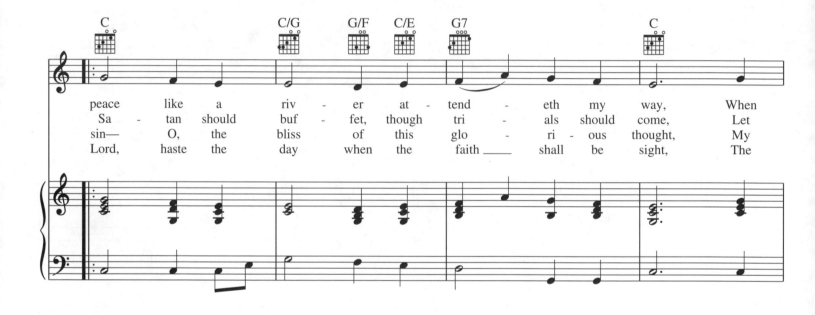

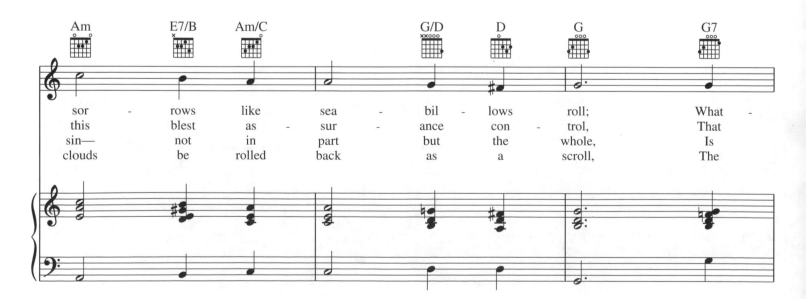

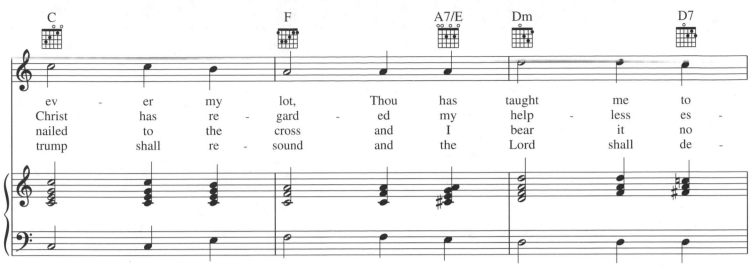

ev - er my lot, Thou has taught me to
Christ has re - gard - ed my help - less es -
nailed to the cross and I bear it no
trump shall re - sound and the Lord shall de -

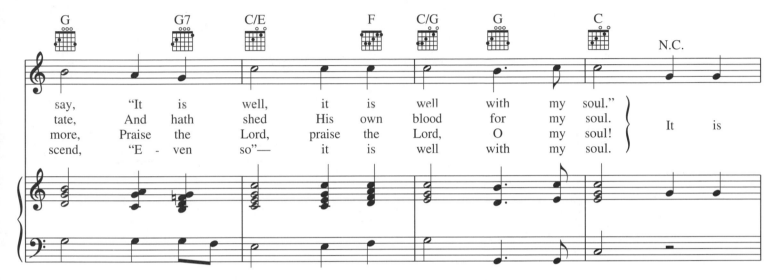

say, "It is well, it is well with my soul."
tate, And it hath shed His own blood for my soul.
more, Praise the Lord, praise the Lord, O my soul!
scend, "E - ven so"— it is well with my soul.

It is

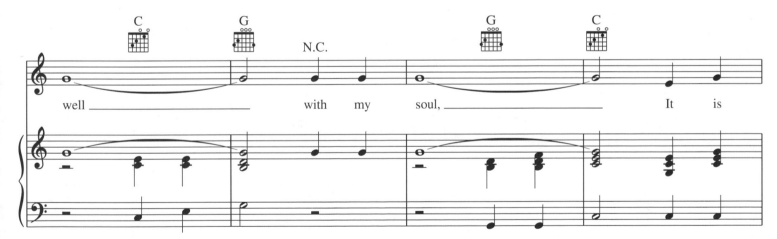

well _____ with my soul, _____ It is

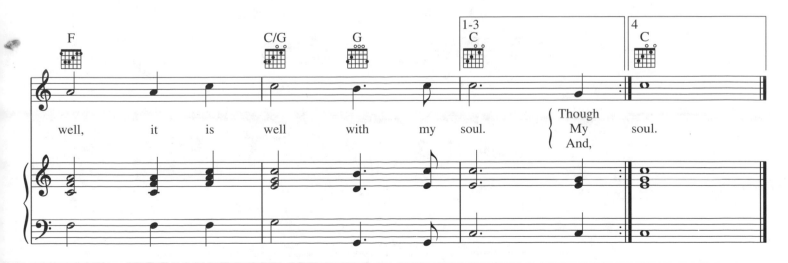

well, it is well with my soul.

Though
My soul.
And,

JESUS WILL STILL BE THERE

Recorded by Point of Grace

Words and Music by ROBERT STERLING
and JOHN MANDEVILLE

Things change, __ plans fail, __ you look for love __ on a grand __
Time flies, ___ hearts turn __ a lit-tle bit wis-er from les-

-er scale. ___ Storms rise, __ hopes fade, __ and
-sons learned. _ But some-times __ weak-ness __ wins, _ and

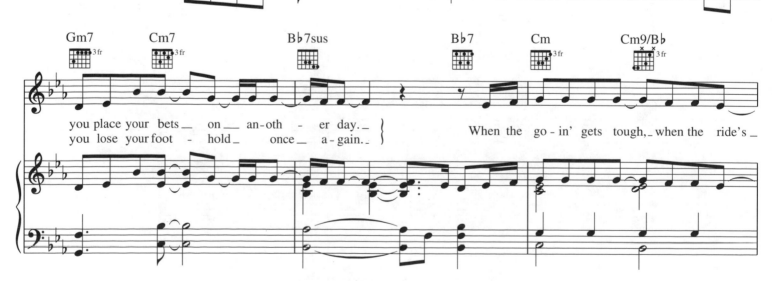

you place your bets __ on __ an-oth-er day. _
you lose your foot-hold __ once __ a-gain. _

When the go-in' gets tough, __ when the ride's __

and you have-n't got _ a prayer, _____ Je - sus will still ___ be ___ there. ___

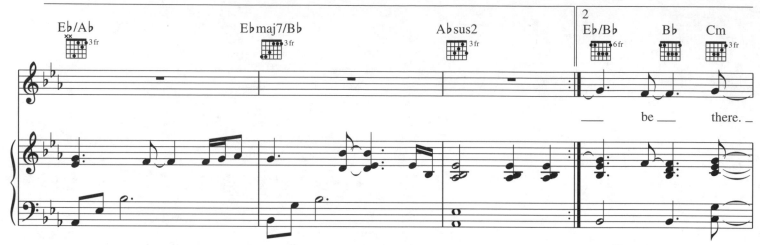

___ be ___ there.

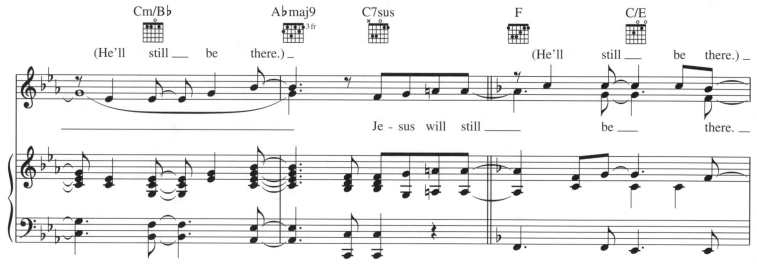

(He'll still ___ be there.) _   (He'll still ___ be there.) _

Je - sus will still _____ be ___ there. _

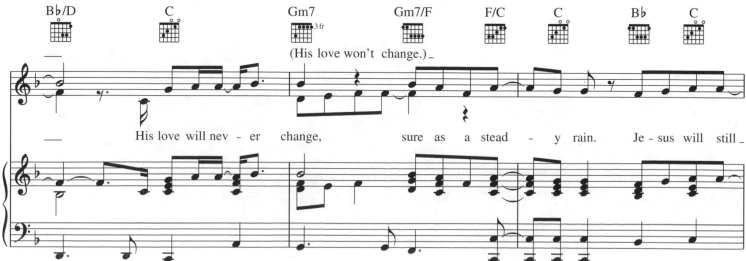

(His love won't change.) _

___ His love will nev - er change,   sure as a stead - y rain. Je - sus will still _

JUST A CLOSER WALK WITH THEE

Traditional
Arranged by KENNETH MORRIS

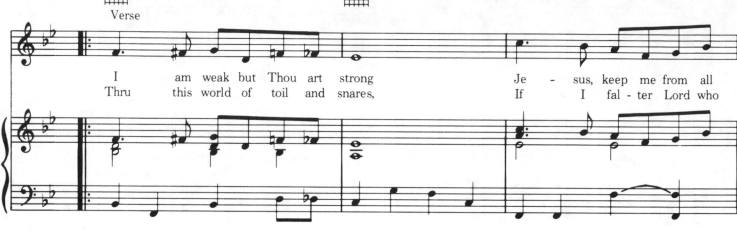

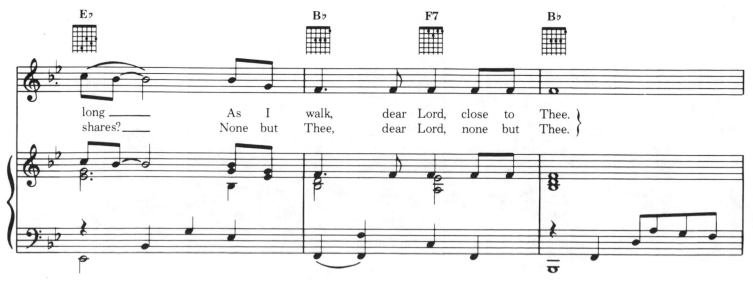

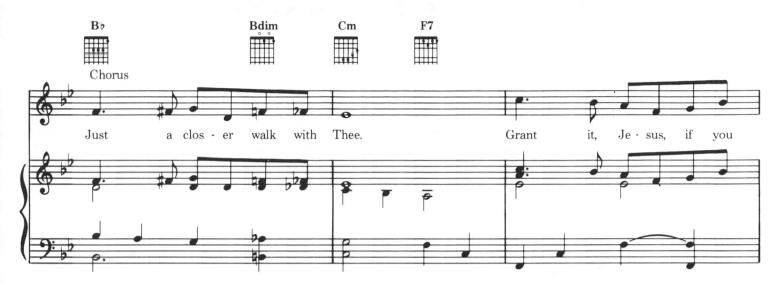

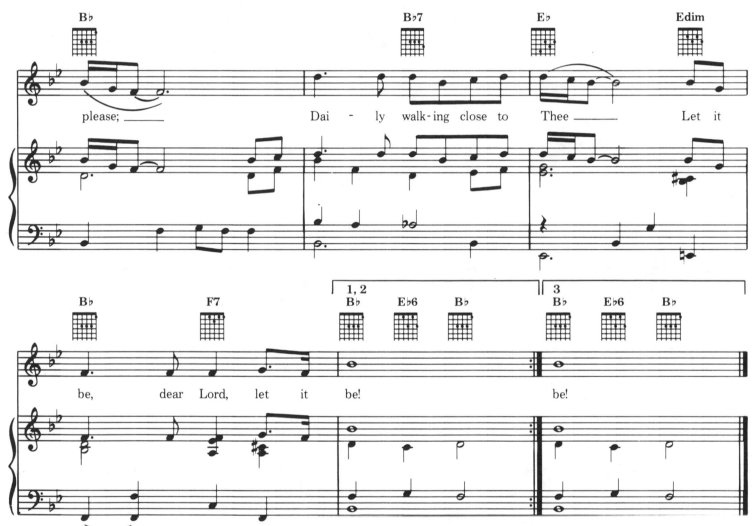

3. When my feeble life is o'er,
Time for me will be no more;
On that bright eternal shore
I will walk, dear Lord, close to Thee.

THE LORD'S PRAYER

By ALBERT H. MALOTTE

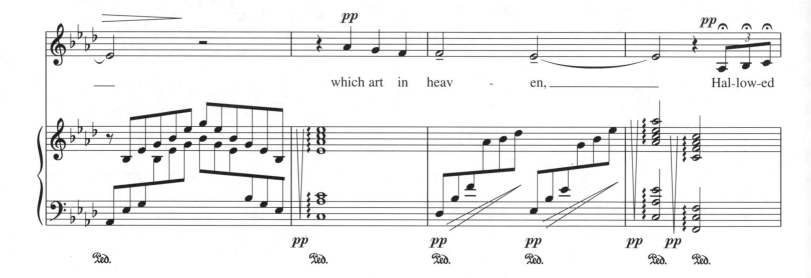

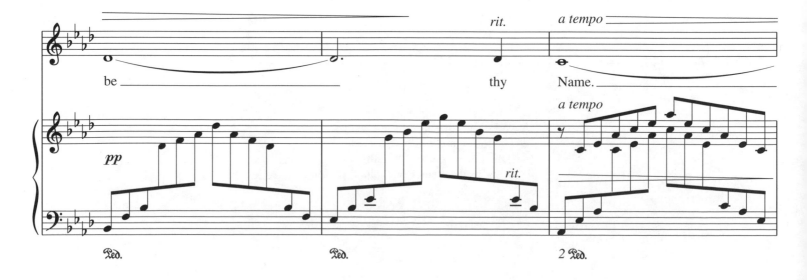

Thy king-dom come.

Thy will be done in earth, As it is in

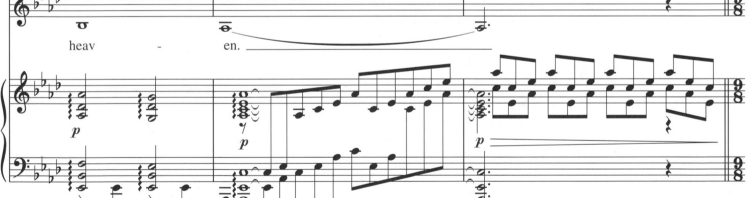

heav - en.

L'istesso tempo

pp molto espressivo e sempre legato

Give us this day our dai - ly bread. And for - give us our debts, _____ As we _____ for-give our debt - ors. And lead us not in - to temp - ta - tion; But de -

Poco meno mosso, e sonoramente

liv- er us from e - vil: For thine is the king- dom, ___ and the pow- er, ___ and the glo - ry, ___ for- ev - - - er. ___ A - men. ___

Tempo I°

rallentando e morendo

MY SAVIOR FIRST OF ALL

Words by FANNY J. CROSBY
Music by JOHN R. SWENEY

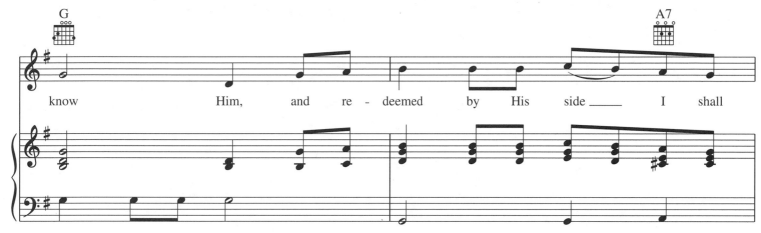

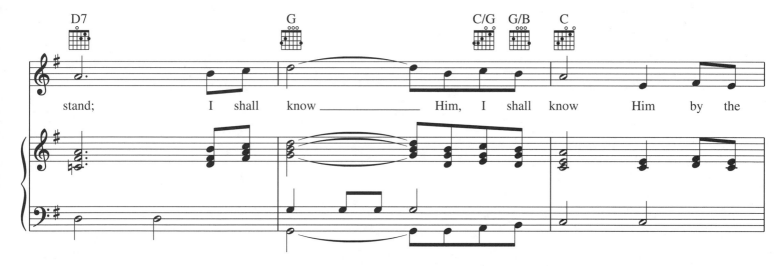

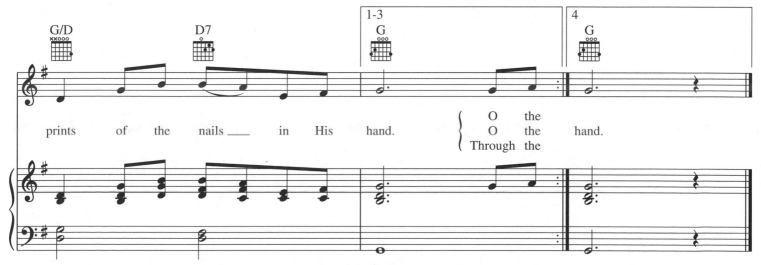

O THAT WILL BE GLORY

Words and Music by
CHARLES H. GABRIEL

When all my la - bors and tri - als are o'er, and I am safe on that

When, by the gift of His in - fi - nite grace, I am ac - cord - ed in

Friends will be there I have loved long a - go; joy like a riv - er a -

beau - ti - ful shore, just to be near the dear Lord I a - dore

heav - en a place, just to be there and to look on His face

round me will flow. Yet just a smile from my Sav - ior, I know,

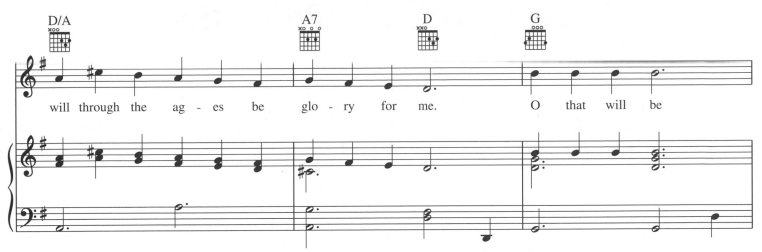

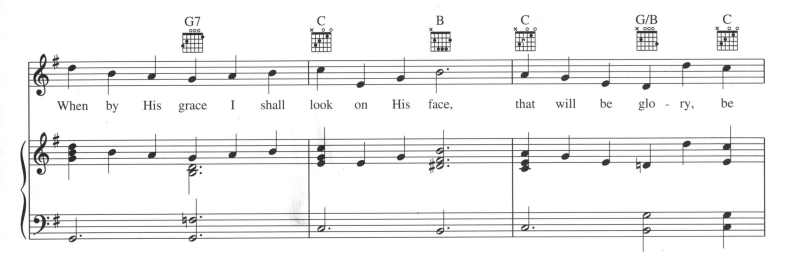

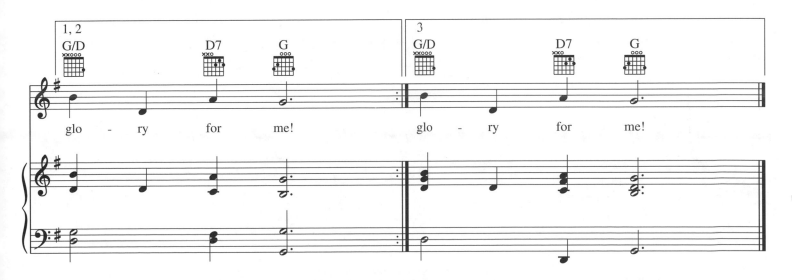

ON JORDAN'S STORMY BANKS

Words by SAMUEL STENNETT
Traditional American Melody

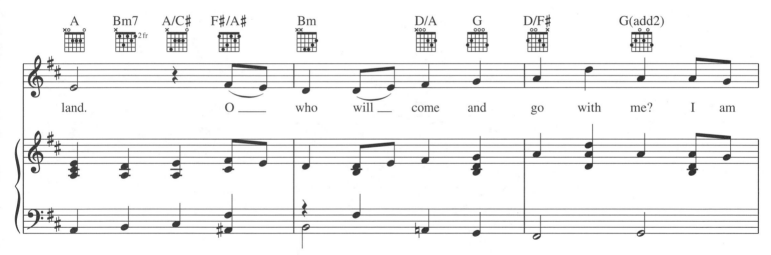

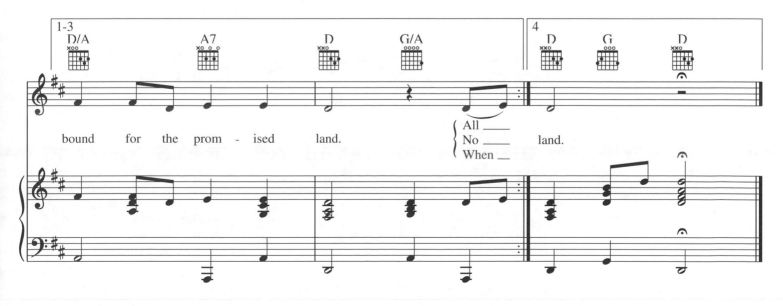

PANIS ANGELICUS
(O Lord Most Holy)

By CÉSAR FRANCK

Poco lento

I dolce

Pa - nis an -

ge - li-cus   fit   pa - nis   ho - mi-num,   Dat   pan - is

coe - li - cus fi - gu - ris ter - mi - num.　　O res mi -

ra - bi - lis　man - du - cat　Do - mi - num,　Pau - per,

pau - per,　ser - vus et hu - mi - lis,　Pau - per,

pau - per,　ser - vus et hu - mi - lis.

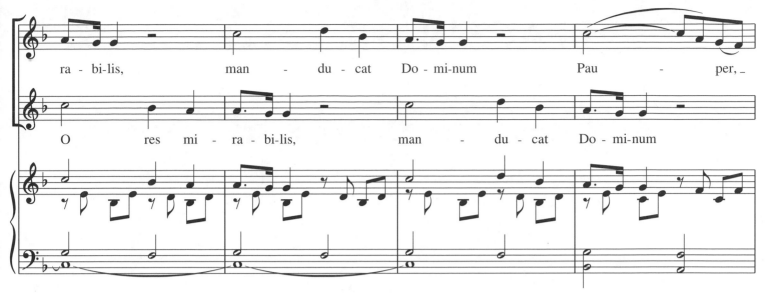

(There'll Be)
PEACE IN THE VALLEY
(For Me)

Words and Music by
THOMAS A. DORSEY

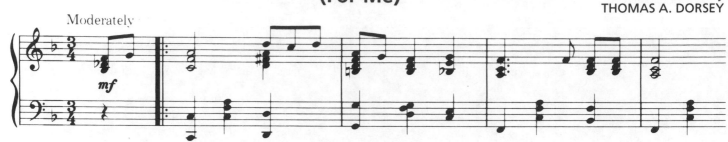

Verse

I am tir - ed and wea - ry, but I must toil on Till the Lord comes to
There the flow'rs will be bloom - ing, the grass will be green, And the skies will be

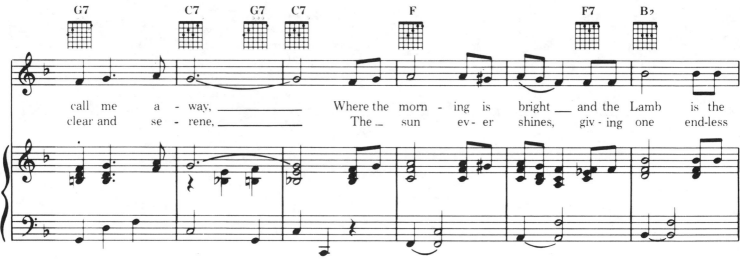

call me a - way, Where the morn - ing is bright and the Lamb is the
clear and se - rene, The sun ev - er shines, giv - ing one end - less

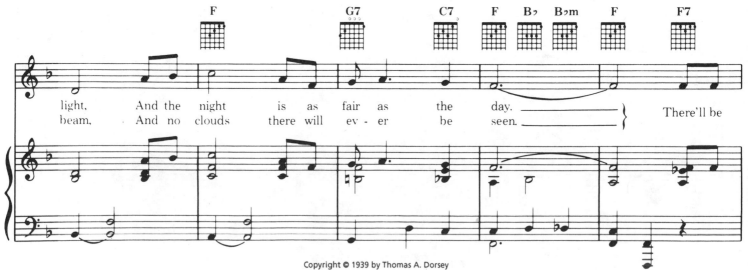

light, And the night is as fair as the day. There'll be
beam, And no clouds there will ev - er be seen.

3. There the bear will be gentle, the wolf will be tame,
   And the lion will lay down by the lamb,
   The host from the wild will be led by a Child,
   I'll be changed from the creature I am.

4. No headaches or heartaches or misunderstands,
   No confusion or trouble won't be,
   No frowns to defile, just a long endless smile,
   There'll be peace and contentment for me.

PRECIOUS LORD, TAKE MY HAND
(Take My Hand, Precious Lord)

Words and Music by
THOMAS A. DORSEY

Slow with Spirit

ROCK OF AGES

Words by AUGUSTUS M. TOPLADY
Altered by THOMAS COTTERILL
Music by THOMAS HASTINGS

TEARS ARE A LANGUAGE

Words and Music by
GORDON JENSEN

Warmly

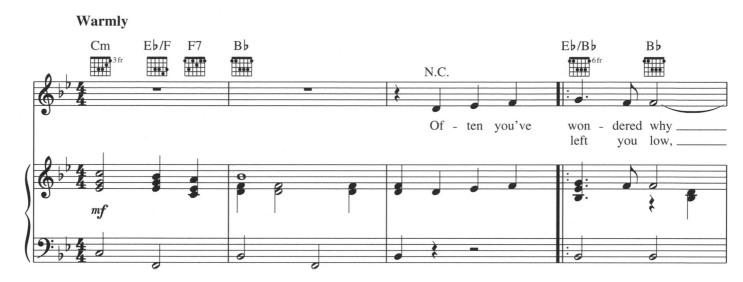

Of - ten you've won - dered why _____ tears come in - to your eyes,
left you low, _____ it caus - es tears to flow;

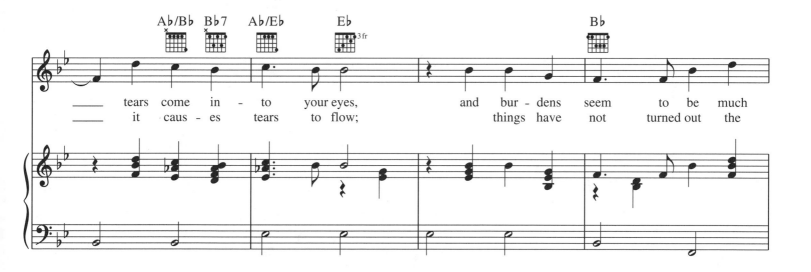

and bur - dens seem to be much more than you can stand.
things have not turned out the way that you can had planned.

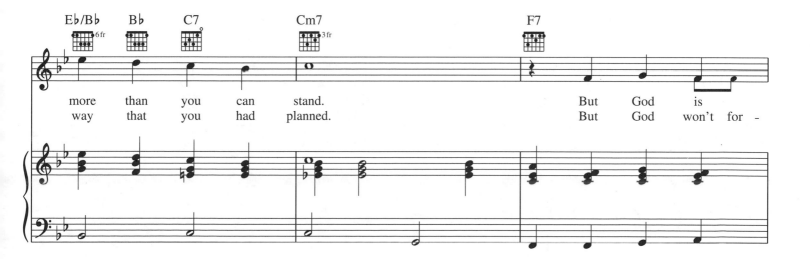

But God is
But God won't for -

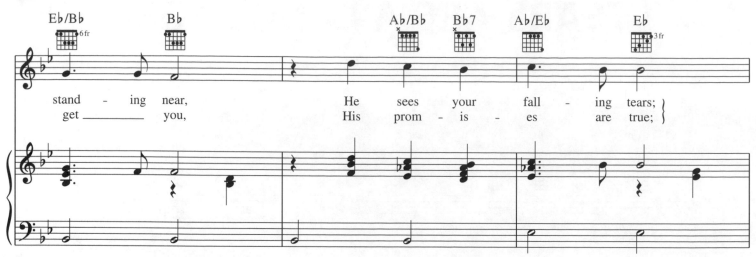

stand - ing near,
get _____ you,

He sees your fall - ing tears;
His prom - is - es are true;

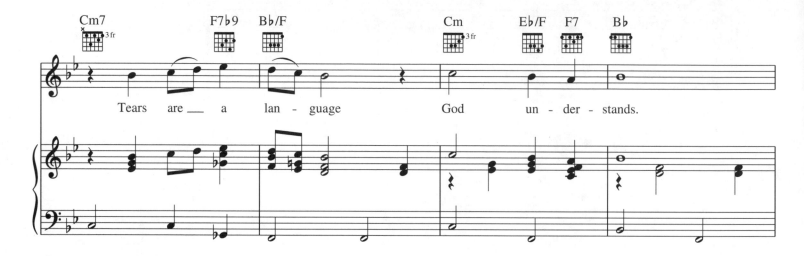

Tears are __ a lan - guage God un - der - stands.

God sees the tears of a bro - ken - heart - ed soul,

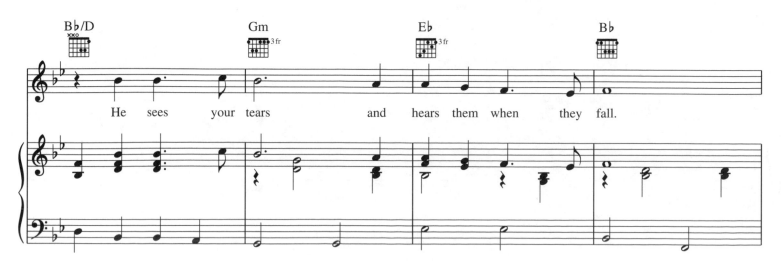

He sees your tears and hears them when they fall.

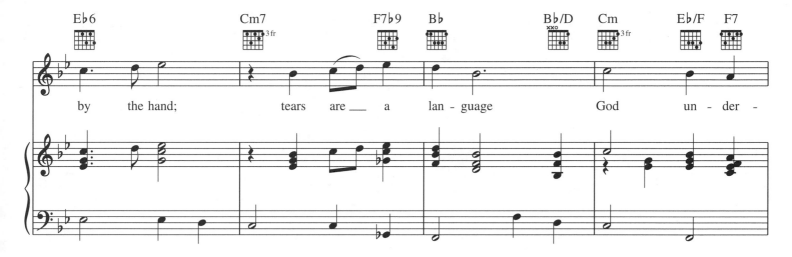

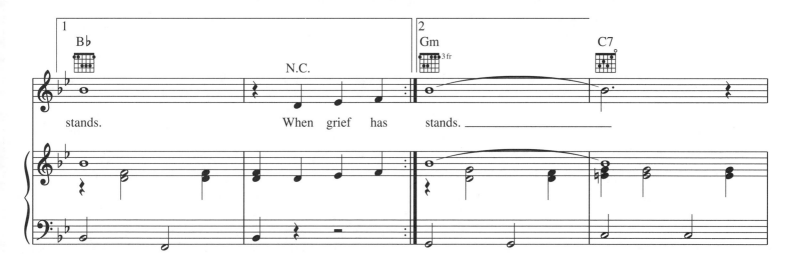

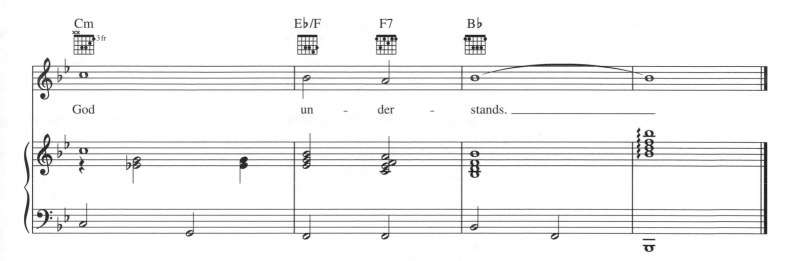

SWEET BY AND BY

Words by SANFORD FILLMORE BENNETT
Music by JOSEPH P. WEBSTER

Cheerfully

There's a land that is fair - er than day, and by
sing on that beau - ti - ful shore the mel
boun - ti - ful Fa - ther a - bove we will

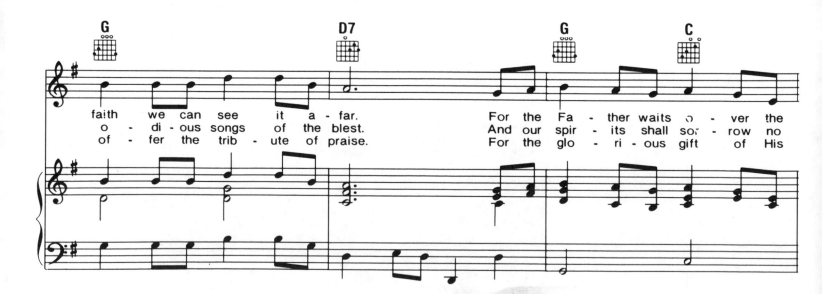

faith we can see it a - far. For the Fa - ther waits o - ver the
o - di - ous songs of the blest. And our spir - its shall sor - row no
of - fer the trib - ute of praise. For the glo - ri - ous gift of His

SWING LOW, SWEET CHARIOT

Traditional Spiritual

Swing low, sweet cha - ri - ot, ___

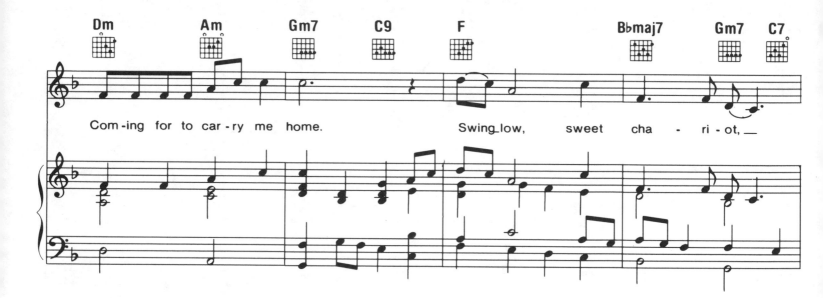

Com - ing for to car - ry me home. Swing low, sweet cha - ri - ot, ___

Com - ing for to car - ry me home. I looked o - ver Jor - dan and
If you ___ get there be -

THEN SHALL THE RIGHTEOUS SHINE

from ELIJAH

By FELIX MENDELSSOHN

heav'n - ly Fa - ther's realm, as the sun,___ as the sun ___ in their
rech - ten, leuch - ten, wie die Son - ne, wie die Son - ne in

heav'n-ly Fa - ther's_ realm.
ih - res Va - ters_ Reich.

Joy on their head shall be for ev - er -
Won - ne und Freu - de wer - den sie er -

last - ing, joy on their head shall be for ev - er - last - ing, and all sor - row and mourn - ing shall
grei - fen. Won - ne und Freu - de wer - den sie er - grei - fen. A - ber Trau - ern, Trau - ern und

flee   a - way,   shall ___   flee _____   a - way for - ev - er.
Seuf -   *zen wird vor   ih - nen*   *flie* - *hen*, ____   *vor ih - nen   flie* - *hen.*

Then,   then ___ shall   the right - eous shine   forth   as the sun   in their heav'n - ly
Dann   wer - den die   Ge-rech - ten   leuch -   *ten,   wie die Son* -   *ne   in ih - res*

Fa -   ther's realm,   shine   forth,   shine   in their heav'n - ly Fa - ther's ___
Va - *ters Reich.*   *Leuch* - *ten,*   *leuch* -   *ten in ih* - *res Vaters* ___

realm, / Reich.
shine forth as the sun _____ in their / Leuch - ten wie die Son - ne in

heav'n-ly Fa - ther's _ realm, then shall the right - eous shine in their / ih - res Va - ters _ Reich, in ih - res Va - ters Reich, in

heav'n - ly Fa - ther's realm. / ih - res Va - ters Reich.

THE TWENTY-THIRD PSALM

By ALBERT H. MALOTTE

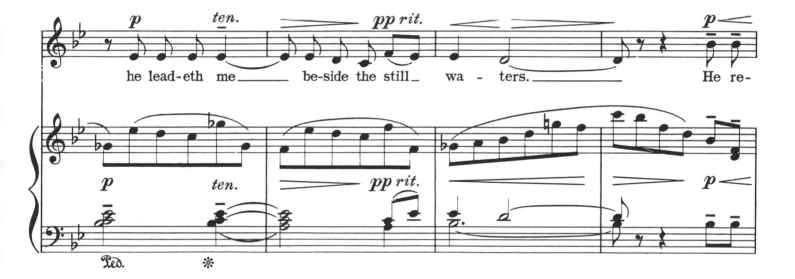

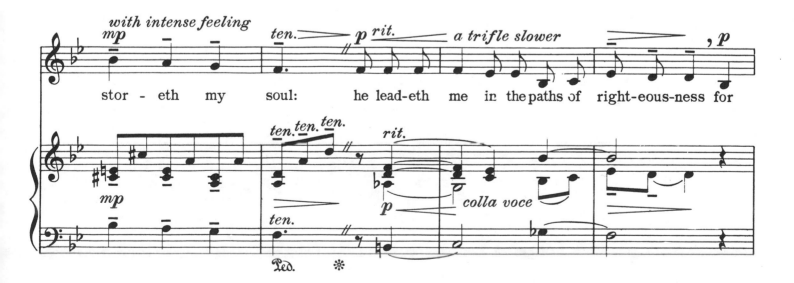

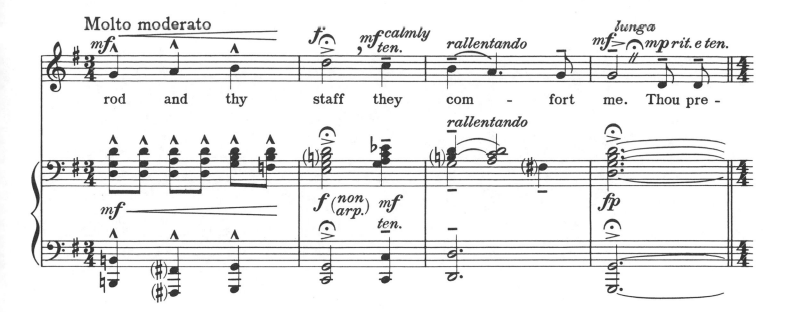

rod and thy staff they com - fort me. Thou pre -

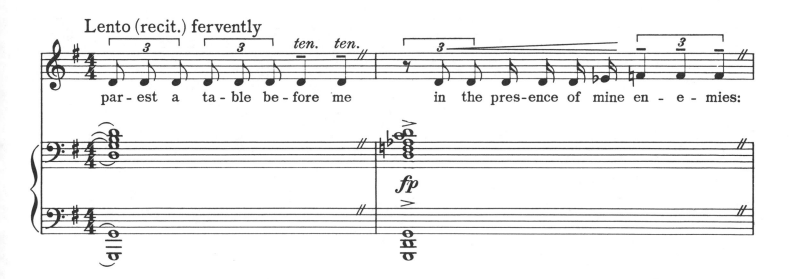

par - est a ta - ble be - fore me in the pres - ence of mine en - e - mies:

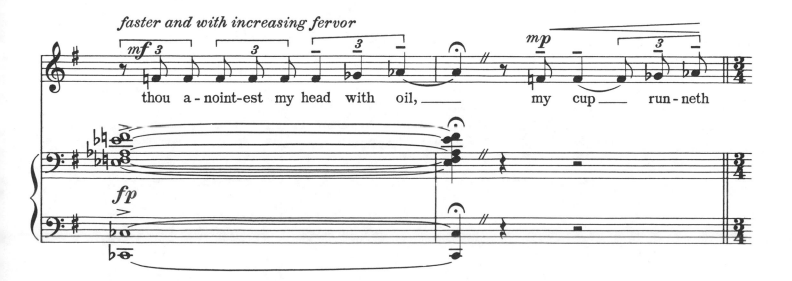

thou a - noint - est my head with oil, ____ my cup ____ run - neth

Più mosso   *rit. e ten.*   **Allegro moderato** (joyously)

o - - ver.   Sure-ly   good-ness and mer - cy   shall

fol - low   me _____   all ___ the days   of   my

Moderato (with exalted confidence)

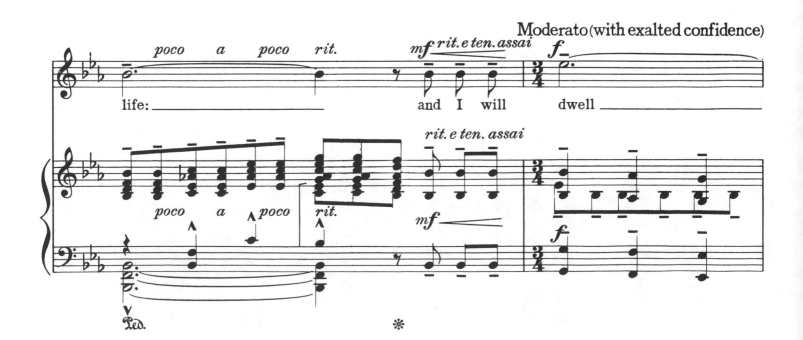

life: _____   and I will   dwell _____

in the house of the Lord for

ev - - er, and ev - - er -

more.

WE'LL UNDERSTAND IT BETTER BY AND BY

Words and Music by
CHARLES A. TINDLEY

1. We are of-ten tossed and driv-en on the
2.-4. *(See additional verses)*

rest-less sea of time, Som-ber skies and howl-ing tem-pests oft suc-ceed a bright sun-shine, In that

land of per-fect day, when the mists have rolled a-way, We will un-der-stand it bet-ter by and

Additional Verses

2. We are often destitute of the things that life demands,
   Want of food and want of shelter, thirsty hills and barren lands,
   We are trusting in the Lord, and according to His word,
   We will understand it better by and by.
   Refrain

3. Trials dark on every hand, and we cannot understand,
   All the ways that God would lead us to that blessed Promised Land;
   But He guides us with His eye and we'll follow till we die,
   For we'll understand it better by and by.
   Refrain

4. Temptations, hidden snares often take us unawares,
   And our hearts are made to bleed for a thoughtless word or deed,
   And we wonder why the test when we try to do our best,
   But we'll understand it better by and by.
   Refrain

WHAT A FRIEND WE HAVE IN JESUS

Words by JOSEPH M. SCRIVEN
Music by CHARLES C. CONVERSE

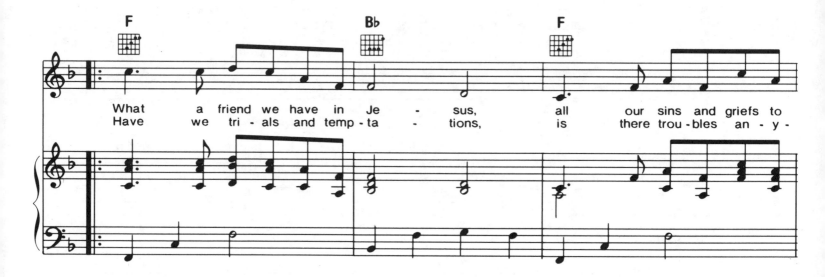

What a friend we have in Je - sus, all our sins and griefs to
Have we tri - als and temp - ta - tions, is there trou - bles an - y-

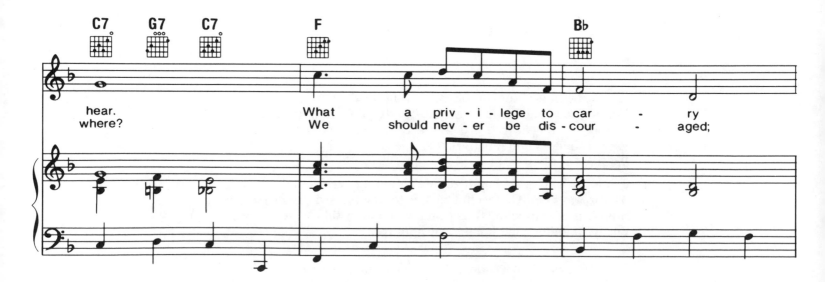

hear. What a priv - i - lege to car - ry
where? We should nev - er be dis - cour - aged;

3. Are we weak and heavy laden,
cumbered with a load of care?
Precious Savior still our refuge;
take it to the Lord in prayer.
Do thy friends despise, forsake thee?
Take it to the Lord in prayer.
In His arms He'll take and shield thee;
thou will find a solace there.

WHEN I LAY MY BURDEN DOWN

African-American Spiritual

bur - den down. ___ Oh, glo - ry, glo - ry! Hal - le - lu - jah!

When I lay ___ my bur-den down. ___ Glo - ry, glo - ry! Hal - le - lu - jah!

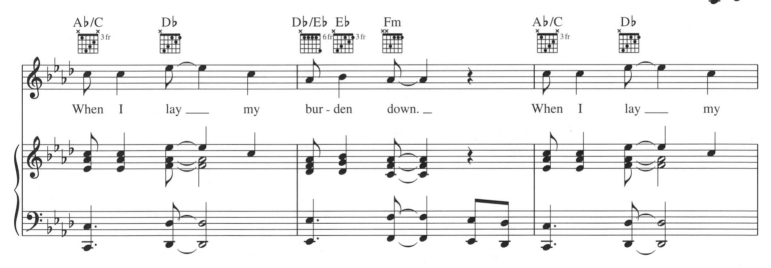

When I lay ___ my bur - den down. ___ When I lay ___ my

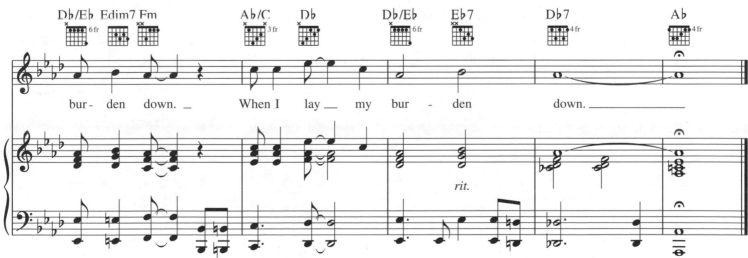

bur - den down. ___ When I lay ___ my bur - den down. _____

WHEN WE ALL GET TO HEAVEN

Words by ELIZA E. HEWITT
Music by EMILY D. WILSON

123

Additional Verses

2. While we walk the pilgrim pathway,
   Clouds will overspread the sky;
   But when trav'ling days are over,
   Not a shadow, not a sigh!
   Refrain

3. Let us then be true and faithful,
   Trusting, serving ev'ryday.
   Just one glimpse of Him in glory
   Will the toils of life repay.
   Refrain

4. Onward to the prize before us!
   Soon His beauty we'll behold.
   Soon the pearly gates will open;
   We shall tread the streets of gold.
   Refrain

YOU'LL NEVER WALK ALONE

from CAROUSEL

Lyrics by OSCAR HAMMERSTEIN II
Music by RICHARD RODGERS

* alternate lyric: hold your head up high